Letters From Georgie

Book 2

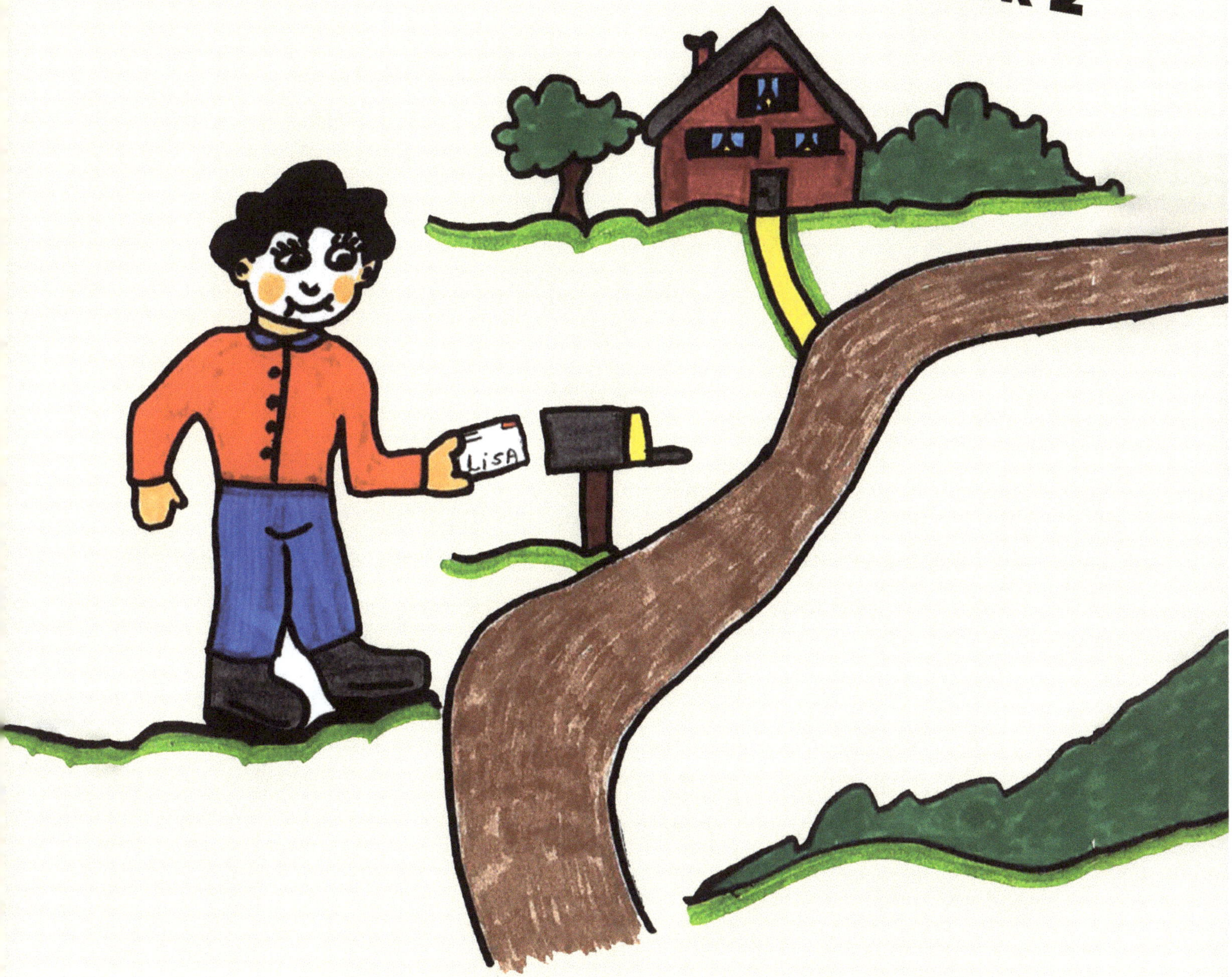

Shelba J. Lynch

Gotham Books

30 N Gould St.

Ste. 20820, Sheridan, WY 82801

https://gothambooksinc.com/

Phone: 1 (307) 464-7800

© 2023 Shelba J. Lynch. All rights reserved. No part of this book may be reproduced, stored in a retrieval system, or transmitted by any means without the written permission of the author.

Published by Gotham Books (February 1, 2023)

ISBN: 979-8-88775-212-9 (P)
ISBN: 979-8-88775-213-6 (E)

Because of the dynamic nature of the Internet, any web addresses or links contained in this book may have changed since publication and may no longer be valid.

The views expressed in this work are solely those of the author and do not necessarily reflect the views of the publisher, and the publisher hereby disclaims any responsibility for them.

Shelba J. Lynch, the Author/Illustrator of this book, was born and raised in a small town in North Carolina. There were six children in the family, four boys and two girls. She was the fourth child in the family, with three older brothers, one younger brother and a younger sister.

After her marriage, she and her husband moved to Charlotte, which is North Carolina's largest city. They raised two sons and a daughter, and still live on the outskirts of the city.

Ms. Lynch declares this book a labor of love. She hopes the children enjoy reading it as much as she enjoyed writing the book.

FORWARD

This book is a true story about a little boy named Georgie.

Most of the dialogue was taken from letters written by Georgie's Mother to her sister, Jean, (who is the author of this book).

Georgie was one year to 3 years old when these letters were written. Georgie refers to himself in this book very often as "Georgie" and as you will see, he was the apple of his Mother's eye.

Georgie is now a grown man. He has been married for a few years, but is still the apple of Mama's eye.

Lisa is Georgie's cousin who lives in another state. She is also the author's daughter and is 6 years older than Georgie.

This Book is Dedicated to:

Richard S. Lynch my husband and special friend of 63 years. He encouraged me all along the way, and convinced me that I had something special in this colorful book.

In Memory Of:

Brian Curtis Lynch our first-born son, who left us much too soon.

Author's Note

I have enjoyed writing and drawing this "Georgie" book. It brings back many fond memories of my nephew, George, when he was a child, and the fun times when he visited us.

Reflections From the South

Being raised in the South (USA) was a wonderful thing. My childhood was very good most of the time, but sometimes a little sad. There were three older brothers, one younger brother and one younger sister in our family.

Reflections of my older brothers are very special to me. They protected me, teased me, let me play with them sometimes, and tormented me (for fun) and loved me.

One memory…
Both my Mother and Daddy worked. Mother worked in a sock factory and Daddy was a carpenter. That left three older brothers to take me to school every day. The school was about a mile away if you walked on the sidewalk. One day, they decided that it would be fun to

take me on a short-cut to school. This resulted in a trip through neighbor's gardens and yards down a steep muddy hill, across railroad tracks, up another red mud embarkment, through more yards, etc.

Needless to say, I had red mud on my shoes and legs, hands and arms, and face and clothes. I was in second grade at the time, and my teacher was upset to see me in such a fix. She helped clean me up, and reported to mother what they had done.

My hometown was one square mile, so we knew just about everyone by name. Many of our friends lived nearby. We enjoyed playing, visiting and doing things with friends at school during summer and winter. I was a cheerleader in the 9th grade, and I played basketball in the 10th, 11th and 12th grades. Loved School!

My Mother and Daddy were very good parents. They taught us the right and Christian way to live. We grew up attending Sunday School and church every Sunday morning.

We walked to church, rain or shine, snow or cold. Growing up in a small town in "The South" was a good thing. I am grateful for my childhood family.

Dear Lisa,

My last letter to you was written when it was still wintertime, and there was a lot of snow on the ground.

Now, it is summertime, and it has been very warm.

We have pretty flowers blooming in our yard, and birds are chirping in the trees.

Mama took me swimming one day when it was hot.

I had to play in the baby pool.

Another day, Mama, Daddy and Georgie went to the zoo. We saw lots of animals.

Some of them were big and scary.

On the 4th of July we went to see some fireworks. They were loud and scary.

I put my hands over my eyes so I wouldn't be able to hear them.

Amy is my little playmate.
We have a really good time playing together.

Yesterday, Amy came to play with me.

Mama let us have a picnic in our back yard.

It will soon be my birthday.
Mama is planning a party for me.

This is like the invitations she is sending to my playschool friends.

Lisa, I hope you will be able to come.

My birthday party was fun. I was two years old.

Seven friends came - got lots of presents - had cake and icecream.

Lisa, I wanted you to
come, but you live too far away.

Thank you, Lisa, for the book you sent me for my birthday present.

Guess I've been a little rough with it, because some of the pages are torn out.

Mama calls me her little "Cookie Crumbler," because I make such a mess every day.

When I'm bad Mama shakes her finger at me, and I shake mine back at her.

I'm Daddy's "buddy" when he is home.

I sit on Daddy's lap to eat supper.

Mama gave me a cup of tea, and I poured it on the kitchen floor.

That was when I found out she really meant business with a little switch she keeps on the cabinet.

Mama says she has to do her housework while Georgie is napping, because I am so demanding and want all her attention.

She said I have been an angel since she showed me "the switch." Georgie runs and hugs and kisses when I see the switch. That makes Mama and Daddy happy.

Last week was a bad one for Lil' Georgie - - - -

I was running through the house and tripped and hit my head on the wall.

It made a big lump on my head.

The next day, I burned my hand on the gas grill -- it was very hot.

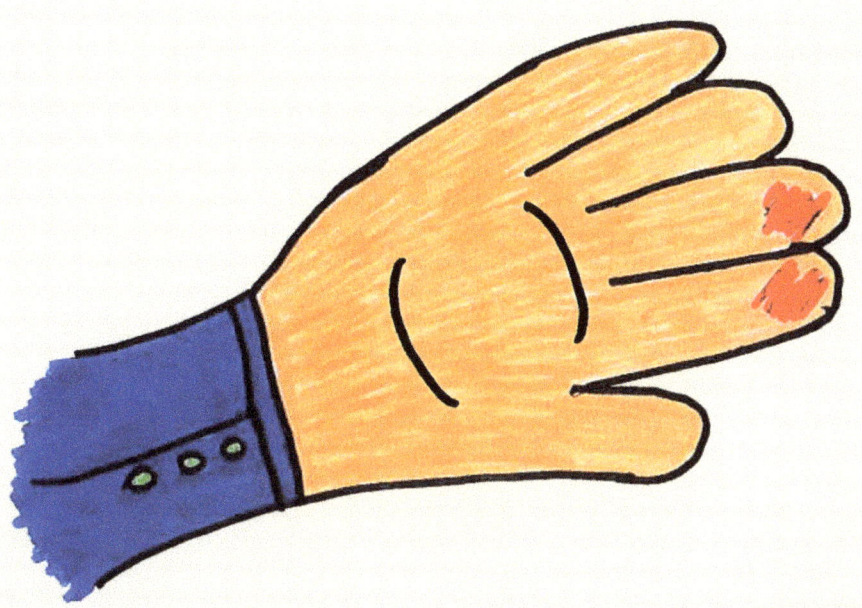

That night, I fell down 3 steps while trying to slide down the stairs.

Skinned my knee.

Georgie started to "Mother's Day Out" school at our church one day a week. I cried a lot the first time, but soon learned to love it.

There are lots of boys and girls and toys to play with at my playschool.

Mama is always trying to comb my hair.

I don't like to have my hair combed, so I run and hide.

Mama and Daddy
plant flowers and cucumbers.

They let me help.

I push my little wheelbarrow.

Mama and Lil' Georgie were on the patio when Daddy came home from work the other day.

He called, "Georgie, where are you?"

I was so excited I jumped up and down, and said, "Outside me, Outside me."

Georgie loves being outside.

I like to ride my tricycle; but when I try to peddle, it always goes backward.

Guess I don't know how to peddle it right.

Lisa, remember when we visited you last summer, and I "broke" Aunt Jean's piano (pulled all the white keys off and spread them on the floor around the bench)?

Mama said Aunt Jean had it fixed, and it looks just like new.

23

One of my favorite things to do in the summer is to chase bugs. I try to catch ladybugs and butterflies.

When it rains, I put on my raincoat and hat and rubber boots, and take a walk in the rain. I love to jump in the puddles and make a big splash. My umbrella keeps me from getting too wet.

My Daddy has promised to take us sailing on the lake the next time you come to visit us.

If Mama will help me, I'll write to you again soon.

       Love,
       Georgie

We received a very special gift on Halloween many years ago. It was a tiny baby girl. We named her "Lisa" Her brothers were 9 and 10 years older than Lisa, so she was pretty spoiled as a child.

We celebrated her birthday by "trick or treating" and inviting friends to a party or going out to dinner. Lisa is Georgie's first Cousin, and they have had many special times together.

Richard and Shelba have, on many occasions, dressed in costumes to attend Halloween parties. It is usually great fun, and "a good time was had by all."

www.ingramcontent.com/pod-product-compliance
Lightning Source LLC
LaVergne TN
LVHW070536070526
838199LV00075B/6788